POEMS BY A 10 YEAR OLD

LOGAN MANNING

Presentation by *BookLeaf Publishing*

Web: www.bookleafpub.com

E-mail: info@bookleafpub.com

ISBN: 9789357619783

First edition 2022

I dedicate my writing to parents who give me as many opportunities as they can, and help to constantly achieve all I can.

ACKNOWLEDGEMENT

My mum always says 'have a go and take every opportunity that you get offered'.

This work is me 'taking the opportunity to have a go'.

PREFACE

This work is an opportunity to 'have a go' and explore a genre of writing that I hadn't previously written in or been exposed to prior to COVID Lockdown.

During 2021 COVID Lockdown, my teacher set weekly poetry tasks to introduce us to, and experiment with new writing styles. I found that I not only enjoyed this experience, (not without the frustration of 'writer's block' and often not knowing where to start), but that I also was able to produce work that I was proud of.

This work is a learning journey as I find, explore and experiment with a variety of styles and structures of poetry.

Rain, Rain, Go Away!

Rain, rain, all day long
Rain, rain, go away!
I want to play, not mope all day
Rain, rain, go away!

Sun, sun, let me run
Dry the puddles, let's have fun.
You let me play, not mope all day
Sun, sun, let me run!

THE CATCH

Red, yellow, orange, pink
Setting from the day.
Ripple here, bubble there,
I think the fish are near...

My tackle box is ready,
Sinkers, hooks and lines.
Long and deep, I aim my cast
Waiting for a bite.

I feel a strong tug,
Reel, reel, reel
Dinner!

SEASONS

Sun
Hot, dry.
Relaxing, surfing, swimming
Singlets, shorts and thongs
SUMMER

Leaves
Trees bare, wind howls.
Colours changing, foliage falling.
Jackets, boots and scarves.
AUTUMN

Cold
Snow, ice.
Raining, snowing, skiing.
Gloves, beanies, coats.
WINTER

New life.
Plants. Animals.
Flowers blooming, animals learning.
Hats, T-shirts, sandals
SPRING   (a Cinquain)

LIONS

Lions.
Laughing lions.
Loving lions.
Lollipop licking lions.
Lazy lions.
Lovely lions.
Lions are cool.

(Alliteration)

BLUE

Blue
Blue looks like the water of the surf.
Blue sounds like waves crashing.
Blue smells refreshing.
Blue tastes salty.
Blue makes me feel energised.
Blue.

(A colour poem)

ULURU

I see a big, red rock
It is a place of silence.
The smell of dust,
It makes my mouth dry.
Under my hands it crumbles.
Uluru.

(A landmark poem)

DANGER

There is fire and smoke
And all that is heard is sirens of emergency
vehicles
My heart pounds in my chest, while I tremble
with fear.
It smells of smoke.
My tongue is dry as sandpaper.
Danger

(An emotive poem)

LOCKDOWN

I am so sad,

Maybe even mad.

My mum drives me crazy,

But, I'll always bring her a daisy.

(A Quatrain)

THE CAMEL

On the road there was a camel,
With a bump that looked like a lump.

He was walking down the street,
Drumming to the beat.
When sand went in his eye.

It made him jump and cry
'Boo Hoo!"

(Nonsense poem)

DOGS AND DUCKS

Dogs lick itchy feet.
Dogs bark and chase the cats.
Dogs steal yummy food.

Ducks dive in water.
Ducks dive catch yummy dinner.
Ducks like to eat fish.

(A Haiku)

THE BBG

The BBG (Big Bad Goblin) is as tall as a house and has razor sharp teeth as yellow as gold! His claws are long, and tough as bricks. His skin is dark green and his beard grown long. Each night he creeps stealthily into the rooms of sleeping children and blows nightmares into their dreams through a straw. He works from twelve, midnight until three am.

(Prose Poem)

HOLIDAY DRIVE

We're going on car trip
Hooray, hooray, hooray!
The car is soo fully loaded
Rooftop to the rims.
Rev! Rev! Starts the engine
...and away we go!

As we drive, more cars I see,
Trucks and fields too.
We play eye spy and eat some lunch
But still no end I see.

I'm getting bored, more lines of white.
Oh, how much more to go?
Finally, I see the lights
of our final destination.
We've been on a car trip
Hooray, hooray, hooray!

Hues of the Rainbow

Red is for roses, fire engines too.

Orange is like sunsets, desert and coral.

Yellow is for sunshine and daisies alike.

Green is for fields and leaves on trees.

Blue is for water - ponds, rivers and streams.

Indigo lies between purple and blue.

Purple is for royalty, violets and gems.

This multicoloured arc is magical to the eye.

The Zoo

At the zoo.
Animals growling,
Purring, laying, swinging high.
On the ground and up, up, in the sky.
Giraffes, monkeys, elephants,
Emus, koalas
What a sight!

(A Septet)

SURFING FUN

On the face of a perfect, glassy wave.
Hard, sharp turns, they're my fave.
I try for an air, but I lose my footing...
SPLASH!

In the water, being spun in the white wash,
it feels like the swish, swash of a washing
machine!
I hold my breath for a second or two,
until I reach the surface.

Another set approaches.
Paddle, paddle, paddle
SPLASH!
Hours of endless fun

LUNCH

My dog was hungry, so he ate my eight sausages!
I made him very full.
While he rested, I read him a fairytale until his
tail wagged.
He fell asleep, but I was bored. Maybe I should
go get my surfboard?
Oh no, it's at home!
Instead I went fishing, to reel in some real fish.
...After all, I didn't get any lunch!

(playing with homophones)

THE BEACH

I see the horizon in the distance.
I taste the salty sea spray in the air.
I smell the pong of seaweed piles.
I hear the waves crashing.
I feel the sand between my toes.
I am ...the beach.

(A poem of the senses)

ADVENTURE

Adrenaline rises.

Diving deep.

Vehicles drive off-road.

Endless experiences await.

Nerve-wrecking anticipation of what is to come.

Traveling to explore new places.

Unusual places to see and things to do.

Reefs of the oceans to explore.

Exciting discoveries and endless memories to create.

(Acrostic poem)